Ella Dawn Creations

Soon To Be Mr. & Mrs.

_____

Wedding Date:

_____

Wedding Planner

WEDDING DATE & TIME:

TO DO LIST:

VENUE ADDRESS:

BUDGET:

OFFICIANT:

WEDDING PARTY:

NOTES & REMINDERS:

Wedding Budget Planner

	BUDGET:	TOTAL COST:	TOTAL PAID:
WEDDING VENUE			
RECEPTION VENUE			
FLORIST			
OFFICIANT			
CATERER			
WEDDING CAKE			
BRIDAL ATTIRE			
GROOM ATTIRE			
BRIDAL JEWELRY			
BRIDESMAID ATTIRE			
GROOMSMEN ATTIRE			
HAIR & MAKE UP			
PHOTOGRAPHER			
VIDEOGRAPHER			
DJ SERVICE/ENTERTAINMENT			
INVITATIONS			
TRANSPORTATION			
WEDDING PARTY GIFTS			
RENTALS			
HONEYMOON			

12 Months Before

- SET THE DATE
- SET YOUR BUDGET
- CHOOSE YOUR THEME
- ORGANIZE ENGAGEMENT PARTY
- RESEARCH VENUES
- BOOK A WEDDING PLANNER
- RESEARCH PHOTOGRAPHERS
- RESEARCH VIDEOGRAPHERS
- RESEARCH DJ'S/ENTERTAINMENT

- CONSIDER FLORISTS
- RESEARCH CATERERS
- DECIDE ON OFFICIANT
- CREATE INITIAL GUEST LIST
- CHOOSE WEDDING PARTY
- SHOP FOR WEDDING DRESS
- REGISTER WITH GIFT REGISTRY
- DISCUSS HONEYMOON IDEAS
- RESEARCH WEDDING RINGS

THINGS TO REMEMBER:

9 Months Before

FINALIZE GUEST LIST

ORDER INVITATIONS

PLAN YOUR RECEPTION

BOOK PHOTOGRAPHER

BOOK VIDEOGRAPHER

BOOK FLORIST

BOOK DJ/ENTERTAINMENT

BOOK CATERER

CHOOSE WEDDING CAKE

CHOOSE WEDDING GOWN

ORDER BRIDESMAIDS DRESSES

RESERVE TUXEDOS

ARRANGE TRANSPORTATION

BOOK WEDDING VENUE

BOOK RECEPTION VENUE

PLAN HONEYMOON

BOOK OFFICIANT

BOOK ROOMS FOR GUESTS

THINGS TO REMEMBER:

6 Months Before

ORDER THANK YOU NOTES

REVIEW RECEPTION DETAILS

MAKE APPT FOR DRESS FITTING

CONFIRM BRIDEMAIDS DRESSES

GET MARRIAGE LICENSE

BOOK HAIR/MAKE UP STYLIST

CONFIRM MUSIC SELECTIONS

PLAN BRIDAL SHOWER

PLAN REHEARSAL

SHOP FOR WEDDING RINGS

THINGS TO REMEMBER:

3 Months Before

MAIL OUT INVITATIONS

MEET WITH OFFICIANT

BUY GIFTS FOR WEDDING PARTY

BOOK FINAL GOWN FITTING

BUY WEDDING BANDS

PLAN YOUR HAIR STYLE

PURCHASE SHOES/HEELS

CONFIRM PASSPORTS ARE VALID

FINALIZE RECEPTION MENU

PLAN REHEARSAL DINNER

CONFIRM ALL BOOKINGS

APPLY FOR MARRIAGE LICENSE

CONFIRM MUSIC SELECTIONS

DRAFT WEDDING VOWS

CHOOSE YOUR MC

ARRANGE AIRPORT TRANSFER

THINGS TO REMEMBER:

1 Month Before

CONFIRM FINAL GUEST COUNT

CONFIRM RECEPTION DETAILS

ATTEND FINAL GOWN FITTING

CONFIRM PHOTOGRAPHER

WRAP WEDDING PARTY GIFTS

CREATE PHOTOGRAPHY SHOT LIST

REHEARSE WEDDING VOWS

BOOK MANI-PEDI

CONFIRM WITH FLORIST

CONFIRM VIDEOGRAPHER

PICK UP BRIDEMAIDS DRESSES

CREATE WEDDING SCHEDULE

THINGS TO REMEMBER:

1 Week Before

FINALIZE SEATING PLANS

MAKE PAYMENTS TO VENDORS

PACK FOR HONEYMOON

CONFIRM HOTEL RESERVATIONS

GIVE SCHEDULE TO PARTY

DELIVER LICENSE TO OFFICIANT

CONFIRM WITH BAKERY

PICK UP WEDDING DRESS

PICK UP TUXEDOS

GIVE MUSIC LIST TO DJ

THINGS TO REMEMBER:

1 Day Before

GET MANICURE/PEDICURE

GIVE GIFTS TO WEDDING PARTY

ATTEND REHEARSAL DINNER

FINALIZE PACKING

GET A GOOD NIGHT'S SLEEP!

TO DO LIST:

The Big Day!

GET HAIR & MAKE UP DONE

MEET WITH BRIDESMAIDS

HAVE A HEALTHY BREAKFAST

GIVE RINGS TO BEST MAN

ENJOY YOUR BIG DAY!

TO DO LIST:

Wedding Events

ENGAGEMENT PARTY:

DATE: _____

LOCATION: _____

TIME: _____

NUMBER OF GUESTS: _____

NOTES:

BRIDAL SHOWER:

DATE: _____

LOCATION: _____

TIME: _____

NUMBER OF GUESTS: _____

NOTES:

BACHELORETTE PARTY:

DATE: _____

LOCATION: _____

TIME: _____

NUMBER OF GUESTS: _____

NOTES:

Wedding Events

BACHELOR PARTY:

DATE: _____   LOCATION: _____

TIME: _____   NUMBER OF GUESTS: _____

NOTES:

REHEARSAL DINNER:

DATE: _____   LOCATION: _____

TIME: _____   NUMBER OF GUESTS: _____

NOTES:

DAY-AFTER BRUNCH:

DATE: _____   LOCATION: _____

TIME: _____   NUMBER OF GUESTS: _____

NOTES:

Wedding Events

CEREMONY REHEARSAL:

DATE: LOCATION:

TIME: NUMBER OF GUESTS:

    NOTES:

PHOTOGRAPHY SHOOT:

DATE: LOCATION:

TIME: NUMBER OF GUESTS:

    NOTES:

RECEPTION:

DATE: LOCATION:

TIME: NUMBER OF GUESTS:

    NOTES:

Wedding Party (the Girls)

MAID/MATRON OF HONOR:

PHONE: DRESS SIZE: SHOE SIZE:

EMAIL:

BRIDESMAID #1:

PHONE: DRESS SIZE: SHOE SIZE:

EMAIL:

BRIDESMAID #2:

PHONE: DRESS SIZE: SHOE SIZE:

EMAIL:

BRIDESMAID #3:

PHONE: DRESS SIZE: SHOE SIZE:

EMAIL:

BRIDESMAID #4:

PHONE: DRESS SIZE: SHOE SIZE:

EMAIL:

NOTES:

Wedding Party (the Girls)

NOTES:

BRIDESMAID #5:

PHONE: DRESS SIZE: SHOE SIZE:

EMAIL:

BRIDESMAID #6:

PHONE: DRESS SIZE: SHOE SIZE:

EMAIL:

BRIDESMAID #7:

PHONE: DRESS SIZE: SHOE SIZE:

EMAIL:

BRIDESMAID #8:

PHONE: DRESS SIZE: SHOE SIZE:

EMAIL:

Wedding Party (the Guys)

BEST MAN:

PHONE: WAIST SIZE: SHOE SIZE:

NECK SIZE: SLEEVE SIZE: JACKET SIZE:

EMAIL:

GROOMSMEN #1:

PHONE: WAIST SIZE: SHOE SIZE:

NECK SIZE: SLEEVE SIZE: JACKET SIZE:

EMAIL:

GROOMSMEN #2:

PHONE: WAIST SIZE: SHOE SIZE:

NECK SIZE: SLEEVE SIZE: JACKET SIZE:

EMAIL:

GROOMSMEN #3:

PHONE: WAIST SIZE: SHOE SIZE:

NECK SIZE: SLEEVE SIZE: JACKET SIZE:

EMAIL:

GROOMSMEN #4:

PHONE: WAIST SIZE: SHOE SIZE:

NECK SIZE: SLEEVE SIZE: JACKET SIZE:

EMAIL:

Wedding Party (the Guys)

NOTES:

GROOMSMEN #5:

PHONE: WAIST SIZE: SHOE SIZE:

NECK SIZE: SLEEVE SIZE: JACKET SIZE:

EMAIL:

GROOMSMEN #6:

PHONE: WAIST SIZE: SHOE SIZE:

NECK SIZE: SLEEVE SIZE: JACKET SIZE:

EMAIL:

GROOMSMEN #7:

PHONE: WAIST SIZE: SHOE SIZE:

NECK SIZE: SLEEVE SIZE: JACKET SIZE:

EMAIL:

GROOMSMEN #8:

PHONE: WAIST SIZE: SHOE SIZE:

NECK SIZE: SLEEVE SIZE: JACKET SIZE:

EMAIL:

Photographer

PHOTOGRAPHER:

PHONE: COMPANY:

EMAIL: ADDRESS:

WEDDING PACKAGE OVERVIEW:

EST PRICE:

INCLUSIONS: YES ✓ NO ✓ COST:

ENGAGEMENT SHOOT:

PHOTO ALBUMS:

FRAMES:

PROOFS INCLUDED:

NEGATIVES INCLUDED:

TOTAL COST:

Videographer

VIDEOGRAPHER:

PHONE: COMPANY:

EMAIL: ADDRESS:

WEDDING PACKAGE OVERVIEW:

EST PRICE:

INCLUSIONS: YES ✓   NO ✓   COST:

DUPLICATES/COPIES:

PHOTO MONTAGE:

MUSIC ADDED:

EDITING:

TOTAL COST:

NOTES:

DJ/Entertainment

DJ/LIVE BAND/ENTERTAINMENT:

PHONE: _____   COMPANY: _____

EMAIL: _____   ADDRESS: _____

START TIME: _____   END TIME: _____

ENTERTAINMENT SERVICE OVERVIEW:

EST PRICE: _____

INCLUSIONS: YES ✓   NO ✓   COST:

SOUND EQUIPMENT:

LIGHTING:

SPECIAL EFFECTS:

GRATUITIES

TOTAL COST:

NOTES:

Florist

FLORIST:

PHONE: COMPANY:

EMAIL: ADDRESS:

FLORAL PACKAGE:

EST PRICE:

INCLUSIONS: YES ✓   NO ✓   COST:

BRIDAL BOUQUET:

THROW AWAY BOUQUET:

CORSAGES:

CEREMONY FLOWERS

CENTERPIECES

CAKE TOPPER

BOUTONNIERE

TOTAL COST:

Wedding Cake/Baker

PHONE: COMPANY:

EMAIL: ADDRESS:

WEDDING CAKE PACKAGE:

COST: _____ FREE TASTING: _____ DELIVERY FEE: _____

FLAVOR:

FILLING:

SIZE:

SHAPE:

COLOR:

EXTRAS:

TOTAL COST:

NOTES:

Transportation Planner

TO CEREMONY: PICK UP TIME: PICK UP LOCATION:

BRIDE:

GROOM:

BRIDE'S PARENTS:

GROOM'S PARENTS:

BRIDESMAIDS:

GROOMSMEN:

NOTES:

TO RECEPTION: PICK UP TIME: PICK UP LOCATION:

BRIDE & GROOM:

BRIDE'S PARENTS:

GROOM'S PARENTS:

BRIDESMAIDS:

GROOMSMEN:

Names & Addresses

CEREMONY:

PHONE:

CONTACT NAME:

EMAIL:

ADDRESS:

RECEPTION:

PHONE:

CONTACT NAME:

EMAIL:

ADDRESS:

OFFICIANT:

PHONE:

CONTACT NAME:

EMAIL:

ADDRESS:

WEDDING PLANNER:

PHONE:

CONTACT NAME:

EMAIL:

ADDRESS:

CATERER:

PHONE:

CONTACT NAME:

EMAIL:

ADDRESS:

FLORIST:

PHONE:

CONTACT NAME:

EMAIL:

ADDRESS:

Names & Addresses

BAKERY:

PHONE: CONTACT NAME:

EMAIL: ADDRESS:

BRIDAL SHOP:

PHONE: CONTACT NAME:

EMAIL: ADDRESS:

PHOTOGRAPHER:

PHONE: CONTACT NAME:

EMAIL: ADDRESS:

VIDEOGRAPHER:

PHONE: CONTACT NAME:

EMAIL: ADDRESS:

DJ/ENTERTAINMENT:

PHONE: CONTACT NAME:

EMAIL: ADDRESS:

HAIR/NAIL SALON:

PHONE: CONTACT NAME:

EMAIL: ADDRESS:

Names & Addresses

MAKE UP ARTIST:

PHONE: CONTACT NAME:

EMAIL: ADDRESS:

RENTALS:

PHONE: CONTACT NAME:

EMAIL: ADDRESS:

HONEYMOON RESORT/HOTEL:

PHONE: CONTACT NAME:

EMAIL: ADDRESS:

TRANSPORTATION SERVICE:

PHONE: CONTACT NAME:

EMAIL: ADDRESS:

NOTES:

Caterer Details

CONTACT INFORMATION:

PHONE: _____   CONTACT NAME: _____

EMAIL: _____   ADDRESS: _____

MENU CHOICE #1:

MENU CHOICE #2:

	YES ✓	NO ✓	COST:
BAR INCLUDED:			
CORKAGE FEE:			
HORS D'OEUVRES:			
TAXES INCLUDED:			
GRATUITIES INCLUDED:			

Menu Planner

HORS D'OEUVRES

1st COURSE:

2nd COURSE:

3rd COURSE:

4th COURSE:

DESSERT:

1 Week Before

	THINGS TO DO:	NOTES:
MONDAY		
TUESDAY		
WEDNESDAY		
THURSDAY		

REMINDERS & NOTES:

1 Week Before

	THINGS TO DO:	NOTES:
FRIDAY		
SATURDAY		
SUNDAY		

LEFT TO DO:

REMINDERS:

NOTES:

Wedding Guest List

NAME:	ADDRESS:	# IN PARTY:	RSVP: ✓

Wedding Guest List

NAME:	ADDRESS:	# IN PARTY:	RSVP: ✓

Wedding Guest List

NAME:	ADDRESS:	# IN PARTY:	RSVP: ✓

Wedding Guest List

NAME:	ADDRESS:	# IN PARTY:	RSVP: ✓

Wedding Guest List

NAME:	ADDRESS:	# IN PARTY:	RSVP: ✓

Wedding Guest List

NAME:	ADDRESS:	# IN PARTY:	RSVP: ✓

Wedding Guest List

NAME:	ADDRESS:	# IN PARTY:	RSVP: ✓

Wedding Guest List

NAME:	ADDRESS:	# IN PARTY:	RSVP: ✓

Wedding Guest List

NAME:	ADDRESS:	# IN PARTY:	RSVP: ✓

Wedding Guest List

NAME:	ADDRESS:	# IN PARTY:	RSVP: ✓

Wedding Guest List

NAME:	ADDRESS:	# IN PARTY:	RSVP: ✓

Wedding Guest List

NAME:	ADDRESS:	# IN PARTY:	RSVP: ✓

Wedding Guest List

NAME:	ADDRESS:	# IN PARTY:	RSVP: ✓

Wedding Guest List

NAME:	ADDRESS:	# IN PARTY:	RSVP: ✓

Wedding Guest List

NAME:	ADDRESS:	# IN PARTY:	RSVP: ✓

Wedding Guest List

NAME:	ADDRESS:	# IN PARTY:	RSVP: ✓

Wedding Guest List

NAME:	ADDRESS:	# IN PARTY:	RSVP: ✓

Wedding Guest List

NAME:	ADDRESS:	# IN PARTY:	RSVP: ✓

Wedding Guest List

NAME:	ADDRESS:	# IN PARTY:	RSVP: ✓

Wedding Guest List

NAME:	ADDRESS:	# IN PARTY:	RSVP: ✓

Wedding Guest List

NAME:	ADDRESS:	# IN PARTY:	RSVP: ✓

Wedding Guest List

NAME:	ADDRESS:	# IN PARTY:	RSVP: ✓

Wedding Guest List

NAME:	ADDRESS:	# IN PARTY:	RSVP: ✓

Wedding Guest List

NAME:	ADDRESS:	# IN PARTY:	RSVP: ✓

Wedding Guest List

NAME:	ADDRESS:	# IN PARTY:	RSVP: ✓

Wedding Guest List

NAME:	ADDRESS:	# IN PARTY:	RSVP: ✓

Wedding Guest List

NAME:	ADDRESS:	# IN PARTY:	RSVP: ✓

Wedding Guest List

NAME:	ADDRESS:	# IN PARTY:	RSVP: ✓

Wedding Guest List

NAME:	ADDRESS:	# IN PARTY:	RSVP: ✓

Wedding Guest List

NAME:	ADDRESS:	# IN PARTY:	RSVP: ✓

Wedding Guest List

NAME:	ADDRESS:	# IN PARTY:	RSVP: ✓

Wedding Guest List

NAME:	ADDRESS:	# IN PARTY:	RSVP: ✓

Wedding Guest List

NAME:	ADDRESS:	# IN PARTY:	RSVP: ✓

Seating Chart Planner

Table #

Table #

Table #

Table #

SEATING PLANNER NOTES:

Seating Chart Planner

Table #

Table #

Table #

Table #

SEATING PLANNER NOTES:

Seating Chart Planner

Table #

Table #

Table #

Table #

SEATING PLANNER NOTES:

Seating Chart Planner

Table #

Table #

Table #

Table #

SEATING PLANNER NOTES:

Seating Chart Planner

Table #

Table #

Table #

Table #

SEATING PLANNER NOTES:

Seating Chart Planner

Table #

Table #

Table #

Table #

SEATING PLANNER NOTES:

Seating Chart Planner

Table #

Table #

Table #

Table #

SEATING PLANNER NOTES:

Seating Chart Planner

Table #

Table #

Table #

Table #

SEATING PLANNER NOTES:

Seating Chart Planner

Table #

Table #

Table #

Table #

SEATING PLANNER NOTES:

Seating Chart Planner

Table #

Table #

Table #

Table #

SEATING PLANNER NOTES:

Seating Chart Planner

Table #

Table #

Table #

Table #

SEATING PLANNER NOTES:

Seating Chart Planner

Table #

Table #

Table #

Table #

SEATING PLANNER NOTES:

Seating Chart Planner

Table #

Table #

Table #

Table #

SEATING PLANNER NOTES:

Seating Chart Planner

Table #

Table #

Table #

Table #

SEATING PLANNER NOTES:

Seating Chart Planner

Table #   Table #

Table #   Table #

SEATING PLANNER NOTES:

Seating Chart Planner

Table #

Table #

Table #

Table #

SEATING PLANNER NOTES:

Seating Chart Planner

Table #

Table #

Table #

Table #

SEATING PLANNER NOTES:

Seating Chart Planner

Table #

Table #

Table #

Table #

SEATING PLANNER NOTES:

Seating Chart Planner

Table #

Table #

Table #

Table #

SEATING PLANNER NOTES:

Wedding Checklist

THINGS TO REMEMBER: **DATE:**   ✓

☐

☐

☐

☐

☐

☐

☐

☐

☐

☐

☐

NOTES:

Wedding Checklist

THINGS TO REMEMBER: DATE: ✓

- [ ]
- [ ]
- [ ]
- [ ]
- [ ]
- [ ]
- [ ]
- [ ]
- [ ]
- [ ]
- [ ]
- [ ]

NOTES:

Wedding Checklist

THINGS TO REMEMBER: DATE: ✓

☐
☐
☐
☐
☐
☐
☐
☐
☐
☐
☐
☐
☐

NOTES:

Wedding Checklist

THINGS TO REMEMBER: **DATE:**   ✓

☐

☐

☐

☐

☐

☐

☐

☐

☐

☐

☐

☐

NOTES:

Wedding Checklist

THINGS TO REMEMBER: **DATE:**   ✓

☐
☐
☐
☐
☐
☐
☐
☐
☐
☐
☐
☐

NOTES:

Wedding Checklist

THINGS TO REMEMBER: DATE: ✓

NOTES:

Wedding Checklist

THINGS TO REMEMBER: DATE:

☐
☐
☐
☐
☐
☐
☐
☐
☐
☐
☐

NOTES:

Wedding Checklist

THINGS TO REMEMBER: **DATE:**   ✓

NOTES:

Wedding Checklist

THINGS TO REMEMBER: **DATE:**   ✓

☐
☐
☐
☐
☐
☐
☐
☐
☐
☐
☐

NOTES:

Wedding Checklist

THINGS TO REMEMBER: DATE: ✓

NOTES:

Wedding Checklist

THINGS TO REMEMBER: **DATE:**   ✓

- ☐
- ☐
- ☐
- ☐
- ☐
- ☐
- ☐
- ☐
- ☐
- ☐
- ☐
- ☐

NOTES:

Wedding Checklist

THINGS TO REMEMBER: DATE: ✓

NOTES:

Wedding Checklist

THINGS TO REMEMBER: DATE:

☐
☐
☐
☐
☐
☐
☐
☐
☐
☐
☐

NOTES:

Wedding Checklist

THINGS TO REMEMBER: DATE: ✓

NOTES:

Wedding Checklist

THINGS TO REMEMBER: **DATE:** ✓

☐

☐

☐

☐

☐

☐

☐

☐

☐

☐

☐

NOTES:

Wedding Checklist

THINGS TO REMEMBER:

DATE:

✓

NOTES:

Wedding Checklist

THINGS TO REMEMBER: DATE: ✓

☐
☐
☐
☐
☐
☐
☐
☐
☐
☐
☐
☐

NOTES:

Wedding Checklist

THINGS TO REMEMBER: **DATE:**   ✓

NOTES:

Wedding Checklist

THINGS TO REMEMBER: DATE: ✓

☐

☐

☐

☐

☐

☐

☐

☐

☐

☐

☐

☐

NOTES:

Wedding Checklist

THINGS TO REMEMBER: **DATE:**

✓

NOTES:

Wedding Checklist

THINGS TO REMEMBER: DATE: ✓

☐

☐

☐

☐

☐

☐

☐

☐

☐

☐

☐

NOTES:

Wedding Checklist

THINGS TO REMEMBER: **DATE:** ✓

NOTES:

Wedding Checklist

THINGS TO REMEMBER: **DATE:**   ✓

☐
☐
☐
☐
☐
☐
☐
☐
☐
☐
☐

NOTES:

Wedding Checklist

THINGS TO REMEMBER: DATE: ✓

NOTES:

Wedding Checklist

THINGS TO REMEMBER: **DATE:**   ✓

NOTES:

Wedding Checklist

THINGS TO REMEMBER: **DATE:**   ✓

NOTES:

Wedding Checklist

THINGS TO REMEMBER: DATE: ✓

☐
☐
☐
☐
☐
☐
☐
☐
☐
☐
☐

NOTES:

Wedding Checklist

THINGS TO REMEMBER:

DATE:

✓

NOTES:

Wedding Checklist

THINGS TO REMEMBER:

DATE:

✓

NOTES:

Wedding Checklist

THINGS TO REMEMBER: DATE: ✓

NOTES:

Wedding Checklist

THINGS TO REMEMBER: **DATE:**   ✓

☐
☐
☐
☐
☐
☐
☐
☐
☐
☐

NOTES:

Wedding Checklist

THINGS TO REMEMBER: **DATE:**   ✓

☐
☐
☐
☐
☐
☐
☐
☐
☐
☐
☐

NOTES:

Wedding Checklist

THINGS TO REMEMBER: **DATE:**

☑

☐
☐
☐
☐
☐
☐
☐
☐
☐
☐
☐
☐

NOTES:

Wedding Checklist

THINGS TO REMEMBER: DATE: ✓

☐

☐

☐

☐

☐

☐

☐

☐

☐

☐

☐

☐

NOTES:

Wedding Checklist

THINGS TO REMEMBER: **DATE:** ✓

NOTES:

Wedding Checklist

THINGS TO REMEMBER: **DATE:**   ✓

NOTES:

Made in the USA
Monee, IL
24 January 2022